Black Existentialism

Autumn Leaves,
And other space oddities

Written By

Julian Thomas

ISBN: 979-8-9906155-6-4 (Hard cover)
ISBN: 979-8-9906155-7-1 (Paperback)
Library of Congress Control Number: 2024939665

Black Existentialism
Autumn Leaves, and Other Space Oddities

"And if all I know how to do is speak, it is for you that I shall speak. My lips shall speak for miseries that have no mouth, my voice shall be the liberty of those who languish in the dungeon of despair. And above all my body as well as my soul, beware of folding your arms in the sterile attitude of spectator, for life is not a spectacle, for a sea of pain is not a proscenium.
A man screaming is not a dancing bear."

-- Aimee Ceasaire

Dedication

This book is dedicated to Tyrone Wilkerson for inspiring a generation. And to Lonny, and all the others that live off the grid.

Special thanks to the jazz greats that formed my poetic flow:

To Coltrane for his tone,
Mingus for his composition,
Bird for his scatalogical bebob expression,
and Miles for his vision.

"Because philosophy arises from awe, a philosopher is bound in his way to be a lover of myths and poetic fables. Poets and philosophers are alike in being big with wonder."

-- St. Thomas Aquinas

"Oh, there's a place deep within my bones, that calls out for something unknown..."

-- The Nightmare Before Christmas

"The day and I grow dark as one."

-- Imura Ryushi

Contents

Foreword

There's a term that gets tossed around a lot these days andI think that is a good place to begin. Decolonize. Decolonize your mind, decolonize this space, decolonized school curriculum, etc. Honestly, I never considered the idea to be inherently intimidating for a white person until I had a graduate school classmate admit to me in a hallway that it did indeed frighten him. Upon deeper consideration, I suppose that's understandable, primarily for anyone still entrenched in the glow of privilege. After all, accepting one's status and seeing imperialism itself as the enemy is the beginning of decolonized thought.

It is time to move beyond phrases like universality, color blindness, and the proverbial "seat at the table." These terms of false inclusiveness only serve to reinforce the illusion of equality and acceptance. This makes it all too easy to overlook underlying issues such as food deserts, unequal medical access, and a lack of economic parity. I don't want a seat at anyone's table if it comes with a lower standard of living and a pay gap. It's not about being against white people, or any people for that matter. It's about fighting oppression anywhere and everywhere it occurs. Mental and economic oppression occur on all levels, and unfortunately, all over the world we are witnessing large scale physical oppression and systemic injustices as well.

In taking the next step against what is now a decently known concept of fighting against the patriarchy, and on a larger scope the dangers of white oppression, decolonizing your mind means turning your back on and rejecting colonial thought itself. And yes, that includes many concepts such as white privilege, male privilege, racism, the gender gap, socio-economic inequity, and lack of inclusion anywhere it takes place. Pair that up with the cultural awareness of black America and you begin to arrive at Black Existentialism.

This book is decolonized poetry.

Black Existentialism is a term that has been used for decades in philosophical writings in the African liberation movement. Many academics point to the work of Franz Fanon in his book *Black Skin, White Masks* and the poignant publication *Decolonizing the Mind* by Kenyan scholar Ngugi wa Tiong'o. In adopting the term for a poetic exploration of American culture, I am claiming this term to apply and explore not only the experiences of black Americans, but all marginalized communities in this country. This counterculture movement includes people of all ethnicities, the often ignored voice of the youth, women, the LGBTQ+ community, as well as the disabled and neurodivergent communities. Anyone who relates to being "the other" is part of Black Existentialism.

And let me be clear here, the role is not to belittle or alienate people of privilege. That's simply not helpful. The process is aimed at pointing out the blinding veil of privilege that allows many good natured people to relax into the man-cave of complacency. The entire argument of "if it doesn't happen to me, then why should I care about it" is not only juvenile, but completely myopic in its shortsightedness. This is a social outlook we simply can not afford.

In short, it is not "us against them". That would only promote the same false dichotomy that the powers that be want for the proletariat. A populace divided is easier to control. Commercialized manipulation through the media is inescapable, but let's not make it easier on them. The idea is to identify these false social narratives so that we can rise above them and come together as one. In all things we are one.

The creative energy that is unlocked when even attempting to decolonize your mind is almost a magical experience. But always and everywhere, it is a spiritual one. Spiritual philosophy goes hand in hand with social commentary, especially when analyzing the ethnic diaspora of American culture. So no matter what the traditional European existentialists may have to say about their internal struggles with conceptualizing the "existence of God", the experience of black existentialism necessitates a spiritual awakening, and indeed on some level, an interaction with and/ or concept of God.

Some of my favorite books growing up were Orwell's *1984*, *Ambiguous Adventure*, the seminal novel on Negritude from Cheikh Hamidou Kane, anything from Amiri Baraka, and all the Sartre I could get my hands on, especially the one titled *Nausea*. For me, traditional existentialism always stood out among other modes of philosophical thought. Existence before essence. It is up to you to define your life. A glaring reality of today is that in this social media world we are largely living the opposite. All that seems to matter is the essence of our lives that we reflect online. But these realities by and large couldn't be any further from the truth. Social media is a tool to be utilized for a specific end, and to be wielded with discretion. My approach to existentialism is less about one's reaction to crisis, and more about carving a deeper understanding of who you are. This book gives you a cross-section of the valleys and peaks of our life.

Truth lives in existence. And existence lives in our truths. Black existentialism is about embracing your otherness. This can only be done by first freeing yourself from the yoke of colonial thought. To exist as your authentic self is the hardest task. To be comfortable with your existence is the life long journey. The process is one of daring to not only be different, but proud of it. Your individuality is your superpower, and that is something that no one can take away from you.

The Poems

"Well 'ya wonder why I always dress in black,
why 'ya never see bright colors on my back.
And why does my appearance seem to have a somber tone?
Well, there's a reason for the things that I have owned.

I wear it for the poor and the beaten down,
livin' in the hopeless, hungry side of town.
I wear it for the prisoner who has long paid for his crime
but is there 'cause he's a victim of the times..."

"...Well there's things that never will be right I know,
and things need changin' every where you go.
But till we start to make a move to make a few things right,
you'll never see me wear a suit of white.

Oh, I'd love to wear a rainbow every day,
and tell the world that everything's okay.
But I'll try to carry off a little darkness on my back,
'til things are brighter, I'm the man in black.

-- Johnny Cash

Elegy for Poets

All the last real poets
That still draw breath

Are too busy
Sparking the revolution

To be famous
From words.

I once knew a poet named Jasmine. She was a real poet, a writer from the core of her being. So she didn't quite fit in at the local poetry hangouts, the open mic's, and the slam venues. She was a real sharp type, like Daria from the old cartoon; angry rant train of thought beat-poetry, that was just plain ol' smarter than you. She couldn't help it, it just was. She taught me many things, but most of all she taught me to trust myself. And to always be true to myself.

Thinking of Jasmine While Reading Bukowski

What happened to the young poets,
      those wild eyed freshly glazed double walled pottery vessels
            of unmitigated passion and radical thought,

The last vestiges of ardor to a porcelain culture
          that has grown *comfortably numb*?

Have they all turned to 'slam'?

Have they grown so desperate for fortune and fame
      that they have forgotten the prerequisite heat,
            or the patience of the granulated press,
            the shoulders upon which they stand?

Such things have no place in pop culture.

What happened to the young poets?

The ones that sit to the back of the cafe, brooding over
      Gwendolyn Brooks, or Baraka, yearning to transcribe
          a classical tone
          into a modern litany of vigor and zeal.

What happened to the young poets?

Have they traded their lotus blossoms and Gill Scott Heron outings
      for a shot at an idol celeb?

Cashed in their Langston and their Nikki Giovanni
for a viral single and an I-Tunes jingle?

Are they gone from us forever?

Or are they just

Deferred?

There's nothing like finishing a new poem. The gentle rocking mental calm after a tumultuous vision quest of a writing storm; it says "*Peace, may the boogie be with you.*" And I dig that. After a long night of churning and gurgling through thought chains and mental tributaries; toiling past the club let-out hours; I love to sit back and admire the first amber peep of the day. "Top of the morning," I usually greet the sun in some such manner. "Time for me to reach slumber."

The Freaks and The Geeks

This is for the nerds, the goths, the gamers and the tweakers.
This is for the emos, the cutters, and the diet pill sneakers,
The cosplay dressers and rave jet setters,
The theatre rats and the weirdos,
And some of the hipsters too.

This is for the trekkies, the fanboys,
The comic-con head liners,
The metal heads, and the deadheads,
And the wannabe rasta crews.
This is for the solo lunchtime cafeteria sitters,
The poets in search of someone,
Anyone to lend them an ear,
And the asian girl who gets
Picked on in class, but keeps
Raising her hand
Anyway.

I do this for the conspiracy theorists and survivalist preppers,
The all-state ball players who secretly want
The lead in West Side Story,
And the former philosophy majors
With their muddy Jeep Wranglers
And their run-down Geo Metros,
So run-down that they only ever
Drive into town once a week to piggyback wifi
And re-stock their coffee grounds and their sugar in the raw.
This is for the stand up comics

With their caustic biting cynicism
And their life worn torn down notepads,
The Irish bar owners with the best Guinness drafts in town
And the irresistible charming eyed girls who work there too.

I do this for the loners, the stoners,
And the comic book donors,
The bar back emcee working his way
Toward one more weekend of studio time,
And the actors, the actors with their never ending
Cycle of euphoric call-backs,
And soul crushing rejections.

I do this for the freaks and the geeks.

I do this for the people like me.

Deep Rivers Run Quiet

Deep rivers run quiet.
It's the shallow waters making all the extra noise,

Churning and gurgling over stony passageways
         and narrow tributaries,
                 growling their liquid disdain,
Reaching and scratching for their place in the dark of the moon.

Ebbing waters with their soft tides
         and their waxing gibbous swell
              toil the night away,

Trickling and scrolling a rippled reflection,
                  reflecting reflection.

Swaying crests and streaming tides in their living water currents
          that lap and languish along with our thought patterns

Spark positive when our heads hang high,
Sag a negative droop when our eyes and our mindfulness tread low.

So keep your head to the sky.

Shallow streams run noisy, but deep rivers drift quiet.
Gently flowing their essence through the depths of cool waters,

The soft breeze in the shadow of the tree.

A current brimming with wisdom
That moves with ninja stealth through dew dropped shores,
           and rests as calm as glass,
               glistening in early morning sun.
  Deep rivers run quiet.

This poem is my ode to Amiri Baraka. May he rest in power. Negritude is the school of writing originated by African authors like Aimé Céasaire, and Cheikh Hamidou Kane; who wrote the seminal Negritudinal novel *Ambiguous Adventure*. Our modern minds are trained to perceive imagery in terms of paleness as pure and good, and darkness as mysterious and bad. Negritude teaches that this is a duality that exists as a colonized language of thought. In their writings the beautiful blackness explores the intellectual and spiritual wonders of the deep. And everything that is shallow, fleeting and toxic is described through metaphors of paleness and white. Most Native American writings explore this perspective as well. The next two poems are specific examples of Negritude.

Post-Modern Negritude
a.k.a. Stand Up Black Man

Black men coming up out of the sea
Rise.
And then,
Walking amongst the populace try to find out
What's good -- "what's good" they be saying,
"Peace, whats the word," dancing in the mist,
Shaking and baking in the modern hustle, the
Industry golden gleam.

Chillaxing with self proclaimed bodega gurus
Nodding and putting their two cents here and
There, as the world continues to burn.
Whats good is the block itself, buzzing and
Nestling its gentrified wave of newbies and wide
Eyed hipsters seeking the latest news.

Word on the street is
"Everything's permissible, but it ain't all good."

And the brothas all inhaling the vibe and the
Sweat and the funk of the city,
Exchanging critiques of the antiquated avant-garde,

Sneaking stolen glances at each other as throngs
Of would-be artisans try to make Beliebers out of them.
What draws them in, their consciousness entangled
With laymen, dreams scattered like restless wolves
In astral forests,
Chasing pranic energy,
Chasing themselves.

A shared hunger entangled with millions of
Countrymen chasing the same fifteen seconds,
And what they thought it could be.

And the brothas, they be shaking, and they be shaking,
But they can't shake the daymares of the populace
So they introduce the funk and splatter drumbeats
Of the Congo and b-sides of Terminator X across
The night scape in fugues,

Scrolls of griot poetry scattered into cyberspace
And cast as sheep amidst the wolves.

"Only the naked can live in the sun", they proclaim
In shouts of laughter and ecstasy, even as the very same
Futile psalms are derided and tossed into the annals of
Twitter-sphere litany,

Water bearers of history
Bundled into formless shades of grey.

Stand up black man.
Stand up and claim the day.

Such hyper-space-cool-daddies as we be homie, we need to
Dream in the real world, and walk in potential. We need to
Collaborate and build and connect ourselves with the spirit
To build, and utilize our brothas and not fear each other, unify
Each other and build foundation for our sistas that they may
Reclaim the pedestal of Mother Earth.

Right now is the word,
And its going down right before your eyes, strong beautiful

Brown eyes emblazoned in the passion and the fierce richness
Of Africa, reflecting the riches of the earth in proud head bobbing
Verses of heartbreak and 808's. Right now is what we have
Because right now is all that is, and right now is the time

To build new melodies of healing and peace.

Never mind the coded subtext in between the lines of song,

All you need

Is the rhythm

That makes it swing.

I'm just going to say it once here and be done with it. The state sanc-tioned murder of innocent black and brown citizens by the current police system is horrific and all too telling of the corrupt state of this republic. If you don't convict cops for killing innocent citizens, it will obviously never stop. As for whitemind, well, it is a state of mind. I'm not against the color white. I'm not against white people. But I am against whitemind. And there's just as many black and brown and all types of people stumbling around with that mentality, even the dispossessed and the other-ed themselves. There's simply no place for it in this post-modern America. There are many ways to be pro-black without being anti-white. I do not believe there is any way to be pro-white without being anti everyone else; including women, the young, the neuro-divergent, and most certainly the poor. Whitemind is a matrix unto itself.

The Protest Poem: Whitemind

This is a protest poem.

This poem is a protest to you, whitemind.

This poem is a protest to imperialism.
Preaching the policies of the bleached power of paleness,
Tricking the advocacy of a system of domination and
Liberty for the few.

Imperialism, you impale me with peril.
Cascading your punishing peripheries to imbeciles of indirection.
Attempting to drown me in your pale sands of ignorance and
Slick me with your trickery,

Lording over the colorful people of the Earth
From a pale ivory tower.

Imperialism, we are impervious to your villainy.
This poem is a protest to bigotry.

Embarking on a journey of self worship and fear of the other.
Imbibing your drunken lust for lordship and obstinate intolerance.
Stealing a landscape of rich dark dreams of creativity
And the beautiful wonders of the deep.

Drowning your potential in a river of false pride,
White water rafting to the American dream
While loosing originality.

Bigotry, you shake hands with lies.
Rerouting imagination into a stale pale desire
To be better than the next.

Taking a tapestry of beautiful colors coast to coast and
Forcing them to fade to your pale pallor of white.
Sucking the very life from your own dreams by
White washing your desires.

This poem is a protest to privilege.
Parading the streets in emperor's clothes
Your false securities give entitled claims to nothing
But laziness and luxury.

Ignorant of your own game
You lower yourself with non-seeing eyes,
Blocking potential by feeding the mind with lies.

Privilege, you benefit no one, not even yourself.
Usurpers of integrity and robbers of authenticity,
Your granted entitlements lead to the agony of self deceit.
In blissful unawareness your blue blooded hopefuls are left
Unprepared for reality from a privilege of ignorance,
Churning away the raw brown grains of our passions
Into ugly white sticks of butter and fat.

I spit in the face of privilege, and
Dream only of the deep richness of heritage and history,
To fill my splayed fingers with the beautiful brown earth,
Reach down into the coal black essence of my passions,
And create new forms of artistic expression;

As God lives in the passion of our work,
While you toil toward your hands of fate.

This poem is a protest to hate.
Swirling and drowning your own potential in the
White man's burden of liquid despair and self-hate;
Chasing it down with little white lies,
While myths of nobility encircle the mind.
False dreams of superiority that stiffen with age
And smother the senses.

Hate is an infection of the eye's lenses.
It deadens the mind the way frost bite
Turns everything stiff and pale.

Hate is a pesky critter, deceptive and frail.

Burrowing into preconceived fears, it coerces and compels
A servant of justice to disperse tickets of cultural genocide
For driving while black,
Or being black while black.

The policy of shoot first, ask questions never,
Where the penalty for murder is paid leave
And early retirement, and apology tours,
And the beat goes on
And the struggle continues.

If you are not part of the solution then you are part of the problem.

This poem is a protest to you, whitemind.

This poem is a protest to the pig.

There's a poet around my block in El Barrio named John 'The Swami' Lesko. He had a big revolutionary poetry event back in the 60's down in The Village, people got arrested and everything, he's the real deal. Swami always has just the right poem for every occasion, just the right haiku of imagery to set your mind at ease, and set your soul at rest. These are Zen style poems in the classic manner of Basho, Issa, Ikkyu, and Ryokan. These poems go out to The Swami.

September Moon

The first full moon of September
Rises with the slow and steady grace
Of a grandmother.

Stretching and lengthening her rays
As she yawns to greet the crisp night air,
She wobbles her pathway upward and onward
To gently crest the moonlit dew,
The misty inverted dawn.

Through slender boughs the silken light
Peers at me with not a twinkle,
But a calm shine.

Shine on my beautiful moon.

Postman of the night,
Sentinel of graveyard shift,

Shine on.

New York Subway Poem

Steel silver casing of sweat,
And grime, and headphones, and two piece suits,

Corrupted artery of city life,
I cling to you.

Like a first time patient to an EKG,
I cling to you.

Like a Julliard hopeful to fresh sheet music,
I cling to you,

For pulse, for passion,
And life line.

I cling, and I sit,
And I sit, and I wonder,

Why, oh why are you never
On time.

This World

This world,
> To what can I liken it?

To Harlem fields
> Lit dimly at dusk
By siren flashes.

I framed this poem all nice and pretty and I gave it to my mother one Mother's Day Sunday. I remember the lady at the framing store came out to tell me I had done a good job, and to say how much she was sure my mother would love it, and to ask me if I was a professional poet. I said, "Why, yes I am. Thank you ma'am."

It's a New Dawn, It's a New Day

It must've been one of those nights.

It must've been one of those jazzy kind of nights,
When the sidewalk sweats with the anxious heart beat
Of a sultry neighborhood.

A no crystal stair kind of neighborhood,
Where the brownstones are resigned to their joy in secret,
Submitting to their lot like the innocent without pardon.
Proud brown Harlem.

Yeah, it had to be one of those nights.

One of those electric funky nights
When The Barrio forgets about the week day's commute,
And the street lamps flicker a syncopated tune.
When the 6 train moves with the exhale of the working class,

The sway of lavender relax,
Like a Coltrane giant step into a steamy bath tub
Soaked in Epsom foot powder,
Enough to handle the work of the spirit,
And the work of the field.

One of those lazy sunset nights,
Where the fading sun sparkles
The East River an amber glow.
And the birds are flying high,
And the breeze is drifting by,

And you know how I feel.

That is how I picture you.
Aquarian Queen in a Concrete Jungle,
Strolling the wisdom of the ages in B-flat.
Shielding me with favor earned decades before
I was a twinkle in your eye,
Or a thought beneath your hat.

The teacher who walks in the shadow of the garden
Gives not of her knowledge,
But rather of her passion for learning,
Her thirst for peace.

She gives inspiration to manic young minds
Like good tidings from the East,

Soothing a troubled past with freshly carved hope
For a sturdier future,

Sculpting foundation
Like granite rock from quicksand.

Plan your work,
Work your plan.

Aquarian Queen in a valley of thickets and thorns,
I would give you the world on a golden platter
Yet still it would not be enough.

It was you that taught me how to lead by example,
And to treat every young soul with respect and concern.

Whether I grew up to be the prince or the healer,
The pastor or the politician.

It was you that taught me how to give without want in return.

To use my gifts not for the sake of acclaim,
But for the chance to be a lighthouse in the dark of the storm.

It was you that taught me how to live by the spirit,
Trusting discernment to leave the salty chaff
And take only the nourishing grain.

It was you that taught me to love without keeping score,
To be the protector, and a pillar of strength.

We've never spoken of these things,
Yet you've shown me all the same.

It's in the way that you speak with dignified grace,
The way that you walk into a crowded room
With noble stature
And discreet nobility.

It's in the way that you lead a classroom with patient tolerance,
And honest enthusiasm that is always exalting,
And never condescending.

It's in the lift of your chin, the resolve in your eyes,
The insight in your voice, and the straightness of a spine
That would never cower to unworthy authority.

The philosopher can explain to you the science of thought,
But he cannot give you his wisdom,
Nor the strength to do what is right.

A master architect may design the most
Fabulous house of all your dreams,
But he cannot make for you a loving home.

The preacher may speak to you of the depths
And wonders of scripture,
But he cannot enter them into your heart
Nor give to you the peace that passes understanding.

Rest assured you have done your job, and done it well.
I pray no misgivings of what if's and would haves
To ever cross your thoughts by day,
Or trouble you at night.

It's my turn to shoulder the burdens
And lead the people.

I will pick up the torch and carry it home.

During one term of grad school, I had an assignment to volunteer at a brain trauma center. They had some of us students sit in on a peer discussion group, and we shared whenever it seemed appropriate. The entire group was so open and willing to talk and share, it was really inspiring. What struck me the most was that they all spoke about the experience of going from being a "normal person" to becoming "the other." This is inspired by a collection of people and stories from that year.

Journaling Through Brain Trauma

I am a brain trauma victim,
My brain works different,
I am not the same as I was before.

The before me,
And the after me;

Two different personas, two altered brains,
But the reflection in the mirror is one and the same.

I am a brain trauma victim,
I'm not like the others
And at work, I am The Other.

I reach out for my favorite mug of coffee,
The one that says Route 66 on the front.

I reach toward the counter but there's nothing there,
And it feels like that old Sartre book I read in undergrad.
What was it?
"Nausea"

Is there nothing there because I misplaced my favorite mug?

There is nothing there because I haven't brewed the coffee yet.

I remember to brew the coffee first,

Favorite mug,
With the Route 66 logo

Flared in gold and black.

And now I remember my favorite flavor,
Hazelnut cream, no sugar.

Is that how I used to take it?

It doesn't matter anymore,
That's how I take it now.

I am not a brain trauma victim,
I'm a survivor.

I am a brain trauma survivor,
My mind works anew, a fresh take on the world.

My personality is different;
Aggressive, or just strong?
It is what it is.

And some friends of mine don't like it,
Some friends of mine can't deal
With the new me.

But patience is a virtue and that starts within, and
And you've got nothing to loose,
You don't loose when you loose fake friends,

Fake friends...

I know that, deep down,
But it's still lonely.

I'm not as quick witted as I used to be.

They call it brain fatigue,
And it makes me tired to organize and think.

I never used to like those cheery eyed, bushy tailed,

Gen Z kiss ups at the office, but now,
Now they're unbearable.
And just because I don't say the words "fuck off"
Doesn't mean I don't want them to.

And every time I hear
Their shrill, chipper, tea kettle voices

I try to hide my level of annoyance.

Does it show?

I think it shows.

Some days are better than others.

I'm different,
I'm not like the others.

I may look normal but I am not,
I am more.

The gift and the curse,
The rose and the thorn.

I think I scared someone at the water cooler
The other day.
I couldn't tell what she was saying,
There were too many people talking at once,

Too many voices to drown out all at once
And I yelled something,

That I won't repeat.

I get sensory overload
And it hurts that other people can't see.

The worst trauma is the ones you can't see.

I am not a victim

I am not a survivor

I am a brain trauma conquerer.
Keeping it real is the only way I can be.

Social norms and blending in

Is just a state of mind,
And rehabilitation takes a very long time.

And if I look annoyed to you,
It's probably because
I probably am.

Through it all,
My greatest weapon is a healthy sense of humor.

I thrive on patience,
I breathe in encouragement,
And I exhale raw truth.

That's all that I have,
That's all that I am.

I miss the person I was,
And I'm excited about
The person I have become.

I'm a conquerer

I'm a conquerer

I'm a brain trauma conquerer.

The Occupy movement lives on... If you don't know, you better ask somebody. I wrote most of this poem on the Metro-North Rail, Hudson Valley Line on the way back to Harlem from a Sunday matinee of the classic play, 'Of Mice and Men'. It was a good show, I played Crooks. Steinbeck is amazing language, so pared down and rubbed raw and true gritted down to a core of just being, just surviving. And of course, it's the tragic story of how we treat the mentally ill. That story lives on as well.

The Ninety-Nine

So
I just stepped out a secondary
Role in a first rate stage production,
'Of Mice and Men,' and I sat down
On the metro north rail and I,

Well,
I got all inspired from reading an excerpt
From Ginsberg's 'Howl' with the rhythm
Of the words and the call of the wild,
And the old school landscape scene.

So
I got all inspired from reading 'Howl'
And I reached for my pad,
No my pad and pencil.
No l.e.d. light needed or
Battery draining, annoying apps to be seen.

So I reached down for my pad
Just to be disappointed once again
By the thoughts it charted
And the pain it gleamed.

Is this the America we changed for,
The world of our shadowy dreams?
We who have dared to tread the murky
Waters of musing back alley open mic's,

And run down theatre spaces,
The wayward unkempt hopes of
Greyhound weary runaways
With dime and a dollar dreams.

We,
Artisans of the underground with our beat box demos
And lazy ramen noodle nights. What do we do it for?
Is it really all about the Benjamin payoff and that
One simple moment of applause,

The
Stopwatch time span of the hot white lights
In our eyes, and a possible standing O?

Those things are nice.

But no,
We do it for the comrades.

We do it for those late night rehearsals
And weary empty stomach backstage
Moments, with their dank musty comfort
And their blue lit haze.

We do it for the secondhand therapy sessions on
Dusty antique couches,
For the cold hard jokes
With their bittersweet, self-deprecating laughter
And their beer soaked, knowing grins.

Those of you lucky enough to ride late
Night trains to small damp basements
Know what i'm talking about.

And if you don't,
These words are poor reflection.
This is the America I fight for.

The unchained melody of the proletariat,
With it's whirlwind of pain, and ecstasy,
And rat raced, lucid, madness.

We are The Ninety Nine
This is our country

This is our song

We work 9 to 5's and 10 to 6's on steamy
Soup drenched dishwashers and
Haggle with line chefs in Hell's Kitchen over
A better price on a nickel bag of funk.

We serve high brows with low morals
And smile through criticism, as they send back
Their overcooked rib-eyes and their
Luke-warm soup.

We are your central park baby stroller warriors,
Treading a path through your child's stiffly somber
Mental development.

We who are raising your toddlers and
Softly inspiring your tweens with a gentle
Word and just the right book recommendation.

Who put out fires on snowy midnight first alerts,
And answered cries of help from wobbly EMT trucks,

Who build sturdier bridges on less sturdy pay scales,
And fix the pot holed streets
Of every metropolitan coast to coast.

We don't want a free ride
All we want is our fair share
But we will fight if we have to
We will fight if we must

We who work the dusty trails from Portlandia
To Baltimore, from Tallahassee to Tucumcari,
And every truck stop
And route 66 mom and pop motel between.

We will fight for this once sacred land
Before it is finally taxed and taken away.

We will fight for our chance to survive the
Onslaught of Orwellian surveillance

And over taxed, uninsured, non-representation.

We will fight

And fight we will.

But you,
All you
Brook's Brother's phonies
And stock market cronies,
You fear-mongering, hate-peddling,
401K squirreling, third generation,
Trust fund inherited
Wall Street corporate goons,
The only question is,

Will you?

Requiem For Grandpa Freddie

What is the measure of the life of a man?
Is it medals and ribbons, placards with gold nameplates,
A closet full of memories and the neckties to match,
Elegant, faded like the lingering sun at dusk.

Is it measured in laughter and shared remembrances,
The telling and re-telling of neighborhood lore
Handed down like winter pants to younger siblings,
Or a secret family recipe for the perfect batch of collards.

Is it calculated with accomplished feats and heroics,
The scores of courageous acts in a youth that saw
Barriers broken down by a black airborne division
As a paratrooper in war torn Korea.

My Grandfather was a man of strong opinions
And broad perspective,
Strong hands, and a strong mind.
An avid student of history,
He spoke of war time conflicts
With the ease and grace of a college professor,
Clarity without condemnation.

A Harlem tenement passes to a new generation,
And still I can hear laughter and shouts outside my window,
Young people set loose to run free in an El-Barrio park,
The rumble of the street with its bustle and its song.

And still I can hear Grandpa,
The resonating chuckle dissecting the latest blunder by Giuliani,
Or the lingering derision that follows every time the Yankees lose,
Again, and again…

My Grandfather was a man of conviction,
His presence a calm and tranquil gust of soothing air,
And his words, though at times sparse,

Would set my mind to undulate,

Like a smooth stone into a still pond.
I never saw him angry.
You measure a man by the people that love him,
By the wisdom he left behind,

The legacy of a life lived with honor and dignity
And without regret.

You measure a tree
By its fruit.

Symphony of a Rose

"He, that dares not grasp the thorn
Should never crave the rose."

-- Anne Bronte

"Beauty of appearance makes its way to the heart
Through the medium of intuitive intelligence called spirit."

-- Hilla Rebay

" ...So close that your hand on my chest is my hand,
So close that your eyes close as I fall asleep."

--Pablo Neruda

"I can not give you the sunset,
But I can give you the night."

-- Erin McCarthy

They call the pain of fleeting joy the song to cheat the rose. The prick of the thorn makes it difficult for the modern mind to enjoy the moment of love. This poem is less of a love poem and more of a conglomerate of thoughts and emotions that boil down to one lyric journey, and the chasers of love encountered along the way. This poem is in the manner of Kahlil Gibran; an archetypal examination of The Rose.

Prelude to a Symphony of A Rose

Her casual walk whispers a tempest
Like a calm shadow that sambas the sun,

But the restless say, "we have wandered and bar-hopped before."
The enamored say, "a rose is a double-edged sword,

Though she boogies your heart strings,
She channels your core.
And with her cries, she will one day ensnarl your soul,
Like a centerfold snake charmer, beckoning your will."

The adepts and the seekers say "nay, she's a pill.
She nourishes our void with warm music and light,
And her radiant presence is a tablet that can soothe the savage night.

Yet when she departs her phantom shadow
Casts an eclipse that darkens even the sun."

In spring say the sowers, "she shall come with the summer drum."

And in the crisp breeze of autumn the toilers say,
"We have seen her treading soft as snow
Among the confessional whispers of holiday wishes."

All of these things have they said of The Rose.

Yet in truth, they spoke not of her,
But of needs unsatisfied.

They spoke not of her essence, but of her tempest,
Not of the life-supporting depths of her cool waters,

But of her tumultuous steam.

They spoke not of the vast wonders of her awesome tidal power,
But of their own thirsts, unsatiated.

The People torture themselves in their quest to capture The Rose.
Better to set it free, and await the triumphant return.

Rather than the stern voice of reason looming through her day,
Seek to be the beacon of wisdom that she calls upon from the dark.

Rather than a whirling frenzy that stirs her passions,
Seek to be her rock of peace.

And on that rock she shall build a kingdom for generations to come.

A Total Babe:
Poem in the Manner of Wayne and Garth

So then I told her, I told her look,
I just gotta make sure that you know
That I know, that you know I know...

If you were a sandwich, you'd be a
BLT... you know,
Babe, lettuce and tomato.

If you were a drink you'd be a
Cosmo-babeton.

Tasty

If you were a breakfast, you'd be...
Babes Benedict.

Very tasty

If you were a car, clearly you'd go to work
As a Babe-M-W,
That's obvious.

But on the weekends,

On the weekends
you'd be a
Harley Babedson
(Gotta keep up that street cred).

And if you were a steak,

You know,
Something I could really sink my teeth into,

Well, of course you'd be
Filet-Babe'gon

And Baby,
I want a bite.

There's something about a nice sixties album on a lazy afternoon. Relaxing with the Lemon Pipers and taking in the calm sway, the mellow groovy vibes... far out, man.

Somber Moon in February Sky

Somber moon shines brightest
In the darkest, coldest sky.

Drop your silver in my tambourine.

Craters etched in ethereal gleam float
Crisp prophecy to the dreams of my Id.

Your curvy slopes beget remembrances,
Shadowy luster of frigid grey lucidity.

Now listen while I play... my green tambourine.

Your call is the song of the night,
The enveloping darkness that illuminates my roots,

A frigid reverse shine
Of native son to terra firma.

Listen while I play...

Hypnotic embrace like the wispy chords of Monk,
All free form and improvised over hazy Ursa Minor.

Watch the jingle jangle start to shine,
Reflections of the music that is mine...

It is you who reminds me to eavesdrop
On the howling wind outside,

And to meditate upon the sterling sleet

Creeping, stacking

Upon my windowpane.
Listen while I play...

The touch of your silver kiss
Thaws my heart,
And seems to shine

For no one else.
She shines
For me.

Bow shaped crescents curved with grace,
Morning frost on brittle grass,
Dew drops like diamonds...

My green tambouri-ine....

-- "Green Tambourine"-- The Lemon Pipers

Cimetière Créole Au Clair de Lune Pale:
Un Poeme de la Nouvelle Orleans

La lune enceinte, la minuit bleu,
La croix concrete brille en lustre ombre demi,

Cimetière créole au clair de lune pale.

Quel que chose dans la cratère
Reflète quel que chose dans l'herbe,

Grise en grise en grise …

Silhouette vêtue de dentelle comme le pouding de pain de bourbon,
Transitoire, un peu d'épice, et séduisante.
Lacet sillouhete habillé reste gravé dans mon esprit,
Comme la vapeur de fumée du repas d'un hiver fait cuire frais,

Comme la brume légère de rosée froide du matin de glace,
Comme Coltrane pendant que vous dormez,
Ou l'amour chaud en matin.

Bonbon de chocolat de lèvres robuste
Comme le baiser de nectarine,
Juteux, nutritif et enivrant.

Lèvres faisant la moue.
Ses baisers ressemblent à la prune de velours grignote,
Intoxication, complet de sang, et un peu effrayant.

Elle est là, et elle n'est pas.

Les genoux cocked dans l'attention profonde,
Elle vous attend.

Creole Cemetery in the Pale Moonlight: A New Orleans Poem

A pregnant moon, in midnight blue,
A concrete cross in half shadowed luster
Shines,

Creole cemetery in the pale moonlight.

Something in the crater
Reflects something in the grass,

Grey on grey, on grey …

Lace clad silhouette like bourbon bread pudding
Transient, a little spicy, and enticing.
Lace clad silhouette remains etched in my mind
Like the steam from the smoke of winter's meal cooked freshly,

As the light fog of cold dew on morning ice,
Like Coltrane's blue note while you sleep,
Or hot love in morning.

Bonbon chocolate lips robust like the kiss from a nectarine,
Juicy, nutritious and intoxicating.

Pouted lips,
Her kisses resemble the velvet plum's gnaw
Intoxicating, bloody, and a bit fearsome,
She is there, and she is not.

Knees cocked in profound attention,
She is waiting for you.

Morning Dew On Damp Grass

Morning dew on damp grass
Greets the sun to face the day,
Sparkles and shines to reflect the dawn.

When the day is young, and the sun spins gold,
Droplets of sparkles grace the pond's surface,
Glistening a liquid army in rippled array.

Closer inspection, or rather,
A widening of the eyes with a delicate
Yet steady gaze reveals a galaxy of stars
That glimmer and flicker in springtime dawn,
Saluting the chill of the break of the day.

Hidden below the surface lies a crowded
Flash photo team of split second rapid fire shine,

Liquid sparklers that sway in amber atmosphere,
Fred Astaire to the haze as they curtsy the air.

A twirl as they shine a pirouette to the sun,

The more you look the more you see
When two walk as one.

And now we shine together.

She's got the sparkle,
That glow, if you will.
Eyes that light up
Like two stolen temple gemstones,
Eyes that go on forever.

She spoke of Kahlil Gibran,
And the little tanned book
In her pretty little backpack.
I spoke of The Celestine Prophecy,
And how I always knew we'd meet

Some day.

Eyes that shimmer in clear reflection like,

Gene Wilder in some old western movie,
Or the good version of the Wonka story.

Yeah, eyes like pure gemstones,
Crystal lamps in an evening moonlight,
Or the last twinkle of Venus just before dawn.

Eyes that remind me of the secret of joy
With their depth and their stillness and
Quiet longing,
Their passion and their calm.

How does the moon become one
With the clear blue sky?

Same way you get to Carnegie Hall,

Patience,
Practice, and
Unyielding devotion.

The hardest loss of all is when it's you're lover and your best friend.
The say time heals all wounds. I say a good poem is even better.

Quantum Entanglement

When summer comes
Can fall be far behind,

Vernal equinox splatters across the
Calendar in amber tones and crisp
Evening air,

Burns the candle at both ends.
Time marches on.

We were always waiting for each other,
Waiting to allow each other to exhale.

There's only one thing in all the known universe
To be infinite density zero volume.

Well, now there's two.

Our love grows where rosemary goes,
Seasoned with a touch of spice, and sipped
With a lemonade in raspberry blue.

And who am I to dare to date
An heiress of the light?

Nay, dating is for youngsters
Like coffee's for closers.

We were never just dating,
There was always way too much
On the line for that.

We were star gazing,
We were soul spelunking,

We were redefining love.
I never thanked you for that.
But now I'm thanking you
With all my heart and all my
Mind and all my spirit.

The hardest loss of all is
When it's your lover and your best friend.

We want things to be the way we want them to be,
That doesn't mean they're bad when they're not.

And now, I see your face behind my eyelids
Before I fall asleep, and when I first awake,

Taunting me for my mistakes,
Teasing me for my mis-steps,
My Texas two-step shuffle through the desert.

But I lost my heart in Oklahoma.

And now
For the first time in my life
I'm ready to seek matrimony.

And now
For the first time in my life
She's already moved on.

Irony?
No, pretty sure this is karma.

But I can't stop thinking about you,
And I know you still think of me.

So please,

Think of me with joy.

Think of our soft kisses
(And the not so soft ones),
The way you squeeze my hand

With that single shared pulse,
Two bodies,

One heart.

And now,
There is a place outside of time,

A place where we're always together,
And its always just before dawn

And your lips
Are on mine.

Besides,
You can never really separate Frigga from Odin.

Thats pantheon level shit,
Thats like separating the air from the sky,
Osiris and Isis,

Some things just can't be done.

The wisdom that lies beyond all words,
That is what you taught me.

When my better half first found me
I didn't recognize her,

But she knew.
She always knew it was me.

I didn't have eyes yet to see,
Ears too freshly clouded with hurt.

That is my only regret.

I took just a little too much time to get my shit together.

No, its not that she hasn't put up with worse jerks than me,
Its just that with me, there was always more on the line.

And thats how it should be,
How its always been.
There's always too much at stake for the roll of the dice,
Too much on the pass line.

No bluffs, no beau stratagems,
Just one move left.
Just giving the heart you've never owned anyways.

This quartz crystal heart of ours
Just needs a lil re-charge,

Just needs to be warmed up,

Earthen elements of two soil benders
To charge an artery and kick-start the core.

You did that for me from the start.

I just wanted a chance to return the favor
In friendship and in vigor,
In moxie and in trust.

There's no quantum leaps in this world.
What's done can not be undone.

But a broken fence can be mended.
Strong wood, barbed wire, and a heavy hammer.

No reason to loose any more cattle from this farm,
No reason to slip through any more cracks.

Together we'll make it out of the desert,
Together we can chant the rain.

A love outside of time is the realest love of all.

It exists without demands, or requests,
Or needful forgiveness.

It just exists,
It just is.

And its not okay,
But when it's all there is
It's nice to dream about once upon a time,
It's nice to remember love.

Was this misplaced faith,
Or just too fabled to believe in?

Either way, it doesn't change the love.

Two bodies,
One heart,

One pulse,
One soul.

Thank you for that.

This candle burns for you.

Black Hole Theory:
A treatise on cosmic love

If science has taught us anything, it's that there's truth in the old adage, as above, so below. Microcosm/macrocosm and all that jazz. So the fable of the theory goes that the only thing comparable to the phenomenon in space known as a black hole is the human soul itself.

But what would it mean to place two black holes in the same vicinity? What would it mean to have two actualized, fully formed, creative maelstroms of raw power and artistic energy and electric charge occupying the same proximity at the same time?

The sacred feminine in fully charged rotation, courageous enough to peer through the gravitational lens distortions of the modern age, with it's matrix of self-aggrandizing social media and its corporate ladders of spirit distortion and unyielding invisible glass ceilings. A cosmonaut of passion de-programmed and free, willing to cross through their own outer and inner event horizons, to gaze with eyes unclouded by fear, or prejudice or enmity.

What would happen to the space where the two event horizons overlap? Infinite density, zero volume next to infinite density, zero volume.

The black tides would collide with such hunger and voracity, that every lonely soul who came into contact would be inspired and moved and charged to create new waves of expression and form. Certainly the shared tidal forces would help calm each other down. Inspiring each other to new heights of intellectual curiosity and creative courage, the theory goes that they would feed on one another, hopefully without the fear of being devoured. For how can you devour something with infinite force, even if you yourself have reached the power of infinity?

My guess is that the gravitational pull would exceed any force in the known or unknown universe. Each celestial body would be bound to one another, an ultimate testament of faith, yielding to the very gravity that allows for infinite freedom. That unstoppable force, *embracing* an immovable object.

But what, I ask, would happen when the two singularities conjoined? A dual nexus. An Einstein-Rosen bridge. No longer a wormhole to the other side, we would then have a fully functioning overpass. This platform (be it digital, audio or live theatrical) would be wide enough to carry the load of those too heavy (or not vibrant enough) to float through a wormhole unhindered.

And what a bridge it would be.

But would those exposed singularities, the uncovered essences of the true power of these lovelorn black hole souls, would they loose their own identity in the foray? Would they have to be willing to loose their former selves in search of that greater truth, that higher connection? Those accomplishments and adventures that are larger than either would have sought to achieve on their own?

Symbiosis; the intimate living together of two dissimilar organisms in a mutually beneficial relationship. One in which I feed you and you feed me, and we grow, together. Massively charged and armed with the truth of the infinite, the other side existing as one with the now and the hereafter. So connected that we would feel each other's yearnings from miles away, through our shared stolen moments of quiet contemplation and quantum foam.

And the world will see, and the world will know.

Brighter than a thousand supernovas, our light would reach the depths of the cosmic black sea found within each lonely soul groping in the darkness for an open mic spot, or an uplifting stage to spread their light and do their thing.

And all we'd have to do is gaze deep into each other's eyes and reflect the mysterious and beautiful abyss of what we already knew was always there.

Cause we're already there.

Autumn Leaves

"The moon, like some albino black hole, draws the light in,
The crescent moon, falling and golden,
And darkens the sky around it erupting in stars,
Word stars, warrior stars, word warriors
                                        assembling
Accents and destinies, moon drawing the light inside."

-- Charles Wright

"If you would be a real seeker after truth,
it is necessary that at least once in your life
you doubt, as far as possible,
all things."

-- Rene Descartes

"Now it reveals its hidden side,
and now the other—thus it falls,
an autumn leaf."

-- Ryokan

Vanity and Self-Pity Go Hand in Hand

Vanity and Self-Pity go hand in hand
Like the leftenant and first capo in one of the five families,
                              separate missions,
                              same godfather,

Plotting and scheming their way to the top,
                    their promotion to advisor of the Id.

Vanity wants the fame,
Cross checking the Ego
          with a freshly cut edge up and his new twitter verification,
                    just the thing to put a little pep in your step,
                              a little glide in your jive...

But Self-Pity, he's a gully dude,
                    keeps it in the gravel pit.

He wants to wallow in his sleeping bag in the corner of the sublet,
          harping on misshapen mishaps and self-fulfilled prophecies,
                lingering on short-comings that only he can see.

Perfection is the OCD little brother of Greatness,
          they're still a close-knit, but they don't talk that much,
                              just busy, I guess.

The apex is never enough, it just keeps spinning
          like a wheel of misfortune without any vowels,
                    like a dog chasing its tail.

Truthfulness demands disclosure,
          and a lie by omission is still a lie all the same.

Its not okay to just do good, you have to do it for the right reason
                    and at the right time.

Yearning for perfection is another form of Vanity
                (like how Fame
                    is just another type of suicide).

We chase our desires
Like a handful of ambition advertisements,
           pursuit of happiness pop ups
                and aspiration bargain discount rates,

Like so many jingles that jangle through our brains,
           spamming our pride with distinction deep fakes,
Never minding the origin from whence they came.

Autumn Leaves

1.

Every season has its sowing, and every sowing has a reaper.
Crisp autumn air with its myriad colors
         and its crackling earth toned leaves,

Contemplations in their maroons and their deep orange blush
         that lead me to reflect on the year with regret and relief.
Always a little bit of both.

The soul becomes dyed with the color of its thoughts.
Yellows and browns in their stained glass musings,
         writing and riding the stiff iron track,
         sculpting hip forms to the fall breeze of its choosing,
A wing and a prayer to pick up the slack.

Autumn leaves but she always finds her way back.

Time dishes out an even-handed retribution.
The wicked flee when none pursueth.

Well, someone's got to pursueth...
It's the reason comeuppances follow those who flee,

It's the reason great things tend to come in three's,
         the skill of the barber, the black fisted comb
         and the spray bottle afro-sheen,

The rose, the knight and the queen,
The mind, the mirror and me,
         keep a damp cloth and an ointment cream
           (scrub it clean, scrub it clean).

Let everything that hath breath praise the lord.
True for seekers, and their poetry.

And me, I'm just a lowly bard,
Just a black man with his poetry, fighting the good fight,

working to transcend.

2.

On the road it's the little things that help you get by,
an extra tasty flavor to a single pack of gum,
Or that footlong hero sandwich with turkey and pepperoni

Slices, cause dammit it tastes good
and thats your only meal for the day anyway,
so you might as well.

Greyhound or Megabus, Amtrak or Metro North Rail,
its all the same after awhile.

And be sure to post some countryside pics,
Gotta keep up those likes, gotta relegate those hits,
but I'm just here to sell some poems,
and maybe open a mind or two along the way.

What they're doing is commodifying culture
in this antisocial media game.

But we all know in this crazy post modern world
What you're saying is only as important as
when you're saying it,
both play second fiddle to how you're saying it.

October is a month for red meat,
Good food, good talk, a steak and red wine in the cool of the day,

A sharpening of the mind and a sharpening of the teeth.
Wind that howls at the desert moon,
the sly whisper of the evil Id,
or the wise reverence of the Supra Ego.

Autumn is the time for night walks with Mingus,
Dreamcatchers that swing in the wind through scented breeze,
sharp wafting pinon cone in crisp evening air,

Relaxed thoughts rolling along like a lazy tumbleweed,
and its all good.

They say the quality of a poem is the quality of the life that lived it.

(Actually I just made that up but it is a cool thing to say).

But how can I name the un-nameless,
How can I put into words the ultimate beauty
              of the wonder of wonders,
                describe the aroma of infinity,
Depict the beautiful shadow in the garden of the tree?

I just write poems, and try to forget about things like
Why leaves always look better in harvest season,
                    or why Nirvana just gets better with age,
                    the band and the transcendent state.

We drift like snowflakes
            floating through a sky of aura shaded grey,
                  tipping along by the thoughts we take,
Giving our dreams to the day.

3.

The Great Almighty has a heck of a sense of humor.
This much we know.
We get to live the examined life,
       and let our stranger than fiction cast humor to the sky,

Good price.

Life is like a new 18 speed.
Silver sun Marco Q5,
Throw in the helmet.
1 queen mattress and box spring, nature's bed
1 full length leather couch / green
1 matching love seat
1 36 inch Panasonic flat screen
Mini papasan chair / brown

Its all for sale.

You've got to let it all go,
And you've got to write it all down.

Cause right now these moments just take hold and grab me,
And then I have to stay up til 4 in the morning,
Or I have to wake up at 4 in the morning
       and hit the writing pad to study my arts,
            my sacred texts.

You've got to write it down and you've got to
Study and reflect in honesty, and purposefully meditate
       and process and run it all down.

Whether its Aimé Césaire or H. Rap Brown,
The Yoga Sutras or St. Thomas Aquinas,
Wu-tang or Coltrane, write it all down.
Whether you study one or the other, its all the same divine light,

Its all the same.
Grinding for the public shine or grinding for the inner glow,
Reaching for the boogie or reaching for the ohm,

Settling in after a long day's work to watch Archer or Bob's Burgers,

its all the same.
Rumi or Neil deGrasse Tyson, Nietzsche or Descartes,
Sam Spade or Shaft, its all the same.

Mysterious ways,
and thats how we like it.

4.

It takes them both you know,
The antiquity store bought status quo classical
And the underground hookup on a thought chop shop.
Dogmatic religion and free spirit mysticism,
                              it takes them both,
                    but most of all, It abhors indifference.

God is worship. God is love. That is all.
Seer, Seeing and Seen.
The audience, the performer and the rhythm of the play itself
                                        in one.

Or Ahab, the ship and the motion of the sea
                    (if you prefer the nomenclature).

We fight to bring ourselves to tolerate other humans
When really we're just lucky the Most High tolerates us at all.

If it were a pronoun, I suppose it'd be a she,
                    cocoon of space/time and all,
                    (don't know where that white bearded
                              guy in the sky came from).

But God is a verb.
And the holy spirit lives in our actions,
                    at least that's the strive, the life long venture.

If all we need is love then why is it so hard to give,
                    and even harder yet to receive?

And why would an all loving Most High allow for this terrible world
                    to have war and racism and bigotry?

Its called free will.
Humans have the freedom to be wack.
I don't judge the greatness of the Big Kahuna upstairs
                    against the mistakes of man.

And trust me, man makes a lot of mistakes,
No judgment there,

we all have our own cross to bear.
As electrons are the purest form of energy,
Ohm is the vibration of the holiest of holies,
dancing in sizzle and form.

The wavelengths, the ripple and the vibration of life,
All in one,
All is one.

5.

Yes, deep rivers run quiet.
It's the tempest and the rocky, jagged raging downdraft
            that runs hard and loud and heavy and free.

You've got to write it all down.
So says Charles Wright,

And so says me.
You've got to write it down Julian,
            love lost memories, sleepless nights, you've got
                        to write it all down.

Short breathed and heart thumping in the cold of the morning,
Misplaced affection from half fooled love dream, watery eyes
From an ex's favorite song, heart thumping blushes to a song
                        from love anew,
                        you've got to write it all down,
Zoned out longing from shadowy college memory,
Nostalgic smile at teen vampire movie, etc., etc...

Every true artist is hyper emotional.
It is the hallowed character unleashed within,
            tumultuous and free, impassioned in daily grind,
            unhindered new age free verse mystic shine.

Your generation will understand the pain.
They feel it as you do,
            write it all down.

You need them both.
The salt of the earth, and the light of the world,
                        you need them both.

The logical foot in the sand, skeptic realism
And the natural born mystic's head in the clouds;
                        you need them both.

If I can talk to the Peace that Passes Understanding
                        like it's my daddy,
Then I can talk to my brother on the block like he's my brother.

And I can talk to Christ like he's my best homie,
                                    our minds are one.

Back in the day, our souls kept time
                    by marching to the pulse of the universe,
Far before we had brains to collect the wisdom in.

I don't believe in a God that needs me to believe in it.

I just pray to the good lord

That God don't never stop

Believing in me.

The Fruit of the Populace

"It is better to illuminate than merely to shine.
Maius est illuminare quam lucere solum."

-- St. Thomas Aquinas

I say unto you, there are fruits of the spirit,
and there are fruits of the populace.
The fruit of the spirit are:
love, joy, peace, patience, kindness, goodness,
faithfulness, gentleness, and self-control.

The fruit of the populace are:
form, color, shape, symbols, shading, symmetry,
metaphor, space, and time.

And most of all, the fruit of the populace is art itself;
creativity, and the will to connect and inspire,
to resonate and disperse truth.
This is the fruit of the populace.

On Form

Form,
Not to be confused with shape,
Is a uniquely perceptual event.

The shape of a thing is set in stone,
Or bronze, or steel, so to speak;
But its Form depends on the Form
Of the mind observing it.

A Form can be a long bold line,
Or a swirling nebulous of ooze,
But always and everywhere
Things have structure;

Whether we can see it or not.

There is no such thing
As a formless painting
Only a formless
Imagination.

On Color

Color creates mood.

Set against its opposite, or even cousin,
Color can take in the random forms
Of the universe
And breathe in life
Or death.

The blending of colors
Is a battle of harmony
And dissonance.
It is this battle that forces us
To bring new shades and tones together.

Color,
A reflection of spectral light,
Has within its range of hues
The whole
Of human
Emotion;

From amber to crimson
To fire engine red,
Moods change,
But it is still
The same
Red.

On Shape

Shape is the gateway to symbolism.

Every culture around the world has its own
Series of shapes that represents the images
And forms in nature that unlock its system
Of beliefs.

Historically, connected to mythology and/or
Religious ideology, shapes can evoke complex
Ideas, or even stories through the most simple
Of patterns and designs. Often masks are used
To represent certain animals or deities.

Since the beginning of civilization cultures
Around the globe have formed statues out of
Every substance known to man. Each figure
Served to be a specific purpose, and had a
Particular meaning. Not until European
Colonization did we get art purely for
Art's sake.

Black Existentialism

On Symbols

Symbols can provide us with something to believe in.

When the military awards someone with a medal,
That piece of tin becomes a force
That commemorates
Courage or honor, etc.

Whether a trophy or a cross
Or a college degree,
We use symbols as physical entities
To project our energy toward.

Its all about the idea behind the symbol.
Never the symbol itself.

They can remind us of a lesson we shouldn't forget,
Or a piece of ourselves we can't let go of.
Whether its a tattoo, or a rainbow in the sky,
Symbols are there so that we do not forget.

On Shading

Shading is perhaps the most subtle of all techniques,
With an emphasis on blending and subtle perception.
Its strength lies in the imagination of the artist,
And that of the perceiver.

Our minds can attach themselves to what we know
A representation should resemble,
And so, an intermingling of
Light and shadow
Takes form.

On Symmetry

Symmetry is perhaps the most simple of all techniques,
And quite possibly, the most essential.

Its strength lies in balance.

The eye feels comforted by the illusion of harmony
Throughout the parts that compose a piece.

Without symmetry the watcher is assaulted with
An overload of dissonance, confusing and scary.

With it, a steady influx of intensity can peacefully
Be taken in.

On Metaphor

See, I use metaphors to break stuff down.
But the real meaning is never the words,
Only the thoughts behind them.
My thoughts, old thoughts, thoughts from nature,
Dark matter, the infinite, everywhere,
But they're just thoughts.
Metaphors help to clarify so like,
I think everyone has two signs to signifying them,
The way they think, and the way they are so like,
I happen to vibe like the earth.
Out of sky, water, fire, or earth, I'm
Earth, thats where you got all those poems,
And well, really the whole flavor of
The first book and so,
I'm earth and I'm the moon.
Like, I dunno...the moon is just me.
So there's what I'll call the cosmological signs too.
Like, sun, moon, and stars,
I know one woman, *she's like a rainbow*,
There's comets, and quasars,
And well, really anything out there,
So metaphors can like break stuff down
To where you can attach a thought and
An idea to something physical
And actual see the thought in action.
Really its just how the human mind works.
Association.

On Space

My favorite space is space.
There is no moment when the air is more energized
Than in the space between audience and performer.
You can almost almost see the vibrations
Sparkling and heavy with rapt attention
Or if its a particularly good performer, even electrifying

I hate it when theatre people talk about space
Like its a Christmas decoration,
"Oh, this is good space, you can hang lights here,"
"Oh, this is bad space, no room for grand parents to sit."

Any space is good space if you know what to do with it.

By taking time for strategic placement of the objects around
One can create a balance of the forces pushing outwards
And those pulling in.

Its not about location, its about
The mindset that we bring to it;
A state of harmony that can occur anywhere
Whether in a black box theatre, or underneath
A swaying willow tree, or simply
On a patch of sidewalk,
A passerby can enter a pact
With the performer,
That for a certain period of time
We will remain free from disturbance
Or distracting thoughts;

And we will allow the space
To engage our minds,
And resonate
The senses.

On Time

Time is a weapon.

If used improperly,
It will strike against you.

If I could somehow choose to grow up in any
Time period in the history of the world,
I would choose now.

If change is the essential property of existence
And time is the fundamental measuring
Stick of that change then
Time is like the tape measure of the universe,

The quintessential ruler of the cosmos.

Yes, time is the measure of change.

Now is the time of the most rapid technological
Advancements that this world has ever seen,
Now is also the time of the world's greatest peril.

For not only do we have the resources
To destroy the entire planet,
But there are entire countries
With the rising animosity and resentment
To set the wheels in motion.

However,
I still contend that right now
Is the best time in history to be alive.

As a grad student, time management is
One of the most important
Aspects of my academic life,

Yet it is the proper management of
Our place in time that will allow

Humans to coexist on this earth,

More or less continue to advance.

Time is the
Grace of the sun across the sky,
The rhythm of the waves in the sea.

It is the way we understand the cycle of life.

Time is to be cherished,
Respected for its unyielding gift of itself.

That doesn't mean you have to go out and
Run a marathon, or climb a mountain
Or even write a rap song

But,
Take a moment to
Every now and then
Reflect on the day.

Stop a moment
And embrace the aroma
Coming from your dinner plate.

In time you'll find
That each moment has a life of its own.

When will we as humans
Finally learn the full complexities of now.

In due time.

On The Black-Hand Side

"He's a complicated man,
and no one understands him but his woman..."

-- Isaac Hayes

"They who dream by day are cognizant of many things
which escape those who dream only by night."

-- Edgar Alan Poe

"We prayed together through hard times,
Smoked hard when it was fitting,
But now we be tappin' breaks
From all them corners that we be bending..."

-- Outkast

To be a poet is to be a revolutionary. In this day and age, any time someone brings a poetic experience to any space, but especially a non-poetry space, it is a performance of activism. We are blessed with the forerunners that forged the paths we walk on, and it is our job to harvest their sowing. We have to call back to the revolutionary poets of yesteryear like Gil Scott Heron, The Last Poets, Pablo Neruda, Nikki Giovanni and Claude McKay, as well as bards of the modern times like Saul Williams and J. Ivey. They planted the seeds. We are the reapers. This book is a call for the poets of America to unite, and elevate, and rejoice in their otherness, and collaborate in the new education and inspiration of the populace.

The Gate Keepers

We are the crypt keepers.
We hold all the keys, and tend to the iron gates.

Stealthily, we glide through wispy
Corridors and mud slicked marble
Passageways, darting to and fro in
Crisp autumn air,
Tending to our flock.

We are the gate keepers,

Watchmen to the cosmic tomb signature of
Chaos from our blood metronome mausoleum,

The midnight marauders of the
Madness within.

Let the
Madness begin.

The Shine

The state of hip hop is the renaissance shine
The mic is the evolution of the grind
The evolution is the mind of the rapper
The rapper is the mic of hip hop classes
The mic is the fight to keep the hood from loosing
And hip hop is the mic of the evolution.

The grind is the evolution of the mic
The evolution is the fight of the mind
The fight is the state of loosing renaissance shine
The state is the fight to keep the hood loosing
The renaissance shine is the mic of the evolution
And the mind is the renaissance shine of hip hop.

Diamond Blood

At sunrise rebel gemstone dealers
Plot bloodshed and thievery
By the glow of the fading moon.

They teach
Moves without form
By dawns early light,
Hijacking the cradle of civilization
For the cut of precious stone.

Ripping son from father
And sweat from bone,

It was you Sierra Leone.

Hold tight to divine heat
Sold price for the swine meat
Shook hands, now they shiesty
Shed blood for a dime piece
Dear God can I find peace

Hold tight to the lost shore
No price on the blood war
Equal ain't in your world
Separate, but I want more,
One day that I touch lord,

Our
Blues song is the black sheep
Roots strong and they pack heat
Blue badge or the white sheet
Dime blood is a fact, we
March on til the shots cease.

Pain shared with the young dead
Lift prayers for the tear shed
Lost tribe, now the dirt red

And we all crave rocks
That were won with the glock
And the shine of the young hard lives,
So we ride for the blood.

Sierra Leone,

It was you that gave us our tradition
Of strength and will to overcome.

A brighter future
Carried on the winds of a savannah breeze.

It was you that linked the bloodshed of our past to
The resurrection of future legacy.

A family's roots traced thru shores of black gold,
Stained with white lies to shade our black truth.

It was you that poured your history of greatness
Into the hollowed out molds of our state side youth.

Condemned to a dismal underworld like hades,
Just to get the flawless cut on sale at Macy's

Robbed clean cause you were cursed with the finest riches,
Lullabies of pain torture your shores for the sake of big business.

They took our families, our homes, our very knowledge of self.
Now we shuffle on BET for your so-called 'conflict free' wealth.

From shanty town to refugee camp, we hear your wounded cry.
A call to action for every black rose that failed to rise.

In your suffering, in your struggle, you are not alone.
United as one, and conquered alone.

We cry freedom for the land of our home.
And we fight

For you
Sierra Leone.

Reality Check

Are you funky brotha
Are you funky or have you
Forgotten the funk
Or are you faking the funk
Has the funk train left you behind
Or are you still holding on to
That which does not groove
That is not the real you
That is the soulless ego
The never-ending appetite of pride
Are you proud of who you are
Or do you fear nonacceptance
Do you need to be part of the crowd
Or can you stand alone
And tall and eager and aware
And raise your fist
And pump it high in the air
Are you funky brotha
Can you dig it
Can you dig that

On Art And Perspective

Au Musée:
(Ars Poetica)

Yesterday I took a trip
To the San Francisco Museum of Modern Art.
A trip I hope I never forget.
For some reason, I'm not worried.

The four most powerful and memorable pieces
Were also the most simplistic in form,

This is no coincidence.

There was a Rothko that was orange on top,
And it faded into a midnight blue,

The ultimate in contrast.

My friend commented that this was because of the way
The vibrant orange seemed to leap form the canvas,
Next to a blue that really seemed blacker than black.

No sooner had I begun to grapple with this concept
Did she notice that within each color on the canvas
Could be found its opposite color interspersed within it.

The blue had specks of orange all through it
And sure enough, in between the strokes of orange
Could be found that deeper than midnight blue.

It was as if all the qualities of the colors
Were strengthened by the presence
Of their spectral opposite.

Damn.
Oh yeah, and that Rothko made me think of a doorway
For some reason.

A door to what I do not know.
Next we saw this blue piece.
And it was just blue.
But the artist had gone to extensive measures
To come up with a particularly vibrant shade of the color,
And it showed.

I was immediately pulled in.

It made me feel like I could just dive into it,
And keep swimming down, down, down...
forever.

My friend's first reaction was that she could soar in it
Until the ends of all time,
Just fly, forever.

Two totally different perspectives,
And yet each one so concretely strong
And true, and real for both of us.

It was immediately encapsulating
In separate but unique ways.

Damn.

The third piece was on the color red.
When she first walked up to it
All she saw was the red.
Soon I pointed out
That you could see your reflection in it
And all my friend could see after that
Was just that,
The reflection.

But it was weird.
It was like seeing through somebody else's eyes.
I took off my hat
And just stood there gaping at this red me,
But for my friend, it was like,
After she saw the new perspective,
She couldn't go back to the old one

No matter how hard she tried.
Damn.
The fourth piece was really special.

What will I be remembered for when I die?
That's what that last piece kept asking me.

The artwork struck me even before I read the caption.
I remember that.

I remember being struck by the sheer energy of the work,
Even though I could see nothing special about it,

The piece had immense texture.
But I didn't want to touch it.

I remember they had a long metal bar marking off
The foot step limits of how close you could get to it,
Rather than the thin black line I'd seen
In front of every other painting that day.
So I inched my toes up to the edge
And peered closely.

The caption revealed it to be what I guess is called
"Cremation art".

This was not the work of an artist,
This was an artist.

The length of the artwork
Counted his years before acquiring a tumor.
The width, the years that followed until his death.

Damn.

It was like I needed to pay last respects or something.
I recall being angered to see the people
Who would just glance at the caption
And move on.
As if this were just another piece of artwork

It wasn't.

He wasn't
To me.
So now I write.
I turn to this pen and this pad for spiritual freedom,
Emotional stability, and intellectual engagement.
Mental spelunking is what I like to call it;
Chipping away at the dark corners of my mentals
To unearth those colorful gemstones
That others call poetry.

They are my children,
No, they are my limbs,
My organs, my lifeblood.

And somehow,
Somehow looking at that piece of artwork
Gave me hope.

Hope that one day in the outdoor playgrounds
And B-day recesses of art history
There's a place for him,
And poets like me
To be remembered.

On Joy

Joy is a secret.
You have to work to find it,
And work to keep it.

The powers that be want to steal it,
That they too may one day
Know its strength and silent validity.

The colonizers may have the power of rage,
But we have the power of joy.

What is possessing the secret of joy?
To be firm and unquestioningly resolute
In the love that feeds it.

To be secure and completely satisfied
In the ease that binds it to you,
And to rest easy in the comfort that it brings.

Possessing joy is at all times a source to attack,
For it is the one thing that can not be stolen away.

They must attack it from within.

They must seek to infiltrate through fears and delusions
And misunderstandings made complicated.

Joy and clarity go hand in hand.
You can not have the one without the other.

Imagine how much joy we would truly find
In the most mundane of every day life
If we truly clearly understood
The magnitude of the creator's master plan.
The peace and the happiness and the life and the light
That is in store for every living creature,

And which already resides

In them.

How we would rejoice at the mere sight of a smile,
Or a sparkle, a stolen moment of truth
Between two passers by.
Joy is the secret that lies hidden among us
And it is the power that lies within.
Seek it, and it will find you.

CO2: A Better Way

The warning of the scientist has got your ear now,
The wear and the tear is affecting all the greenhouse.
We're pumping carbon dioxide in to the sky,
A blanket in the atmosphere, trapping the heat in side.

The king of this planet, we rule it, ride the iron horse.
The plants and animals, what's keeping them from dying off?
We 'bout to hit the tipping point world-wide,
A heat wave worse than Chicago in '95.

Lack of snow in northern states, farmers barely growing fruit,
Category 5 storms have tripled since '82
Warmer water is what feeds hurricanes and typhoons.
Got us fearing war on terror when the levee breaking loose.

We keeping secret lyrics and grinding to get the pay,
And clocking our spirits until they all annihilate.
Flood us with under covers, double speak our minds away,
There's got to be a better way, there's got to be a better way.

We break it down and making it pound with God-phrase.
And screw it down and send it out where Al Gore stay.
We cleaning the system, got us shining a brighter day,
There's got to be a better way, there's got to be a better way.

We oil addicted can see the planet heat up,
A flood is raping and pillaging Indonesia.
A broken promise already stole your soul,
Kyoto Treaty, when he pledged emission control.

We're elevating carbon output to the wrong number,
Cause what we're dealing with is worse than just a hot summer.
A hundred insects that only live in the tropics,
Disease is the topic, the migration they'll never stop it.

And now they wanna tell me Al Gore's crazy,
Half the population lives fifty miles from the sea.
The polar ice melts, the ocean grows three hundred feet,

They're already adding sand to Miami South Beach.

We keeping secret lyrics and grinding to get the pay,
And clocking our spirits until they all annihilate.
Flood us with under covers, double speak our minds away,
There's got to be a better way, there's got to be a better way.

We break it down and making it pound with God-phrase.
And screw it down and send it out where Al Gore stay.
We cleaning the system, got us shining a brighter day,
There's got to be a better way, there's got to be a better way.

Wind farms, geothermal plants ain't new,
Its busses in Sweden that run on bio-gas fuel.
We gotta live smart, not bigger to spread raucous,
Better batteries for cars, biodiesel for the truckers.

Could generate the power with a wind turbine
But the corporate fiscal profit's more important than our lives.
And federal assistance is stiffer than rigor mortis,
They can give 'em tax breaks for alternative sources.

The only ray of hope is from mayors who made agreements;
Sell pollution credits for meeting emission ceilings.
A greenhouse initiative, Seattle to the bay,
True leaders of the day, there's gotta be a better way.

We keeping secret lyrics and grinding to get the pay,
And clocking our spirits until they all annihilate.
Flood us with under covers, double speak our minds away,
There's got to be a better way, there's got to be a better way.

We break it down and making it pound with God-phrase.
And screw it down and send it out where Al Gore stay.
We cleaning the system, got us shining a brighter day,
There's got to be a better way, there's got to be a better way.

Haters Hate Because They Hate Themselves

Haters hate because they hate themselves,
Just like scammers fake
Because they can't create wealth.
But if you happen to be comrades, or dating one,
You must help them overcome whatever it is
They hate within themselves.

You must do this
Diligently,
Or one day
That person will turn on you,
Often in a violent fit of rage.

The Matrix will always call out to you,
Beguile you to come back, and to seek
Fame, and to relinquish your Negritude,
And become a normie, and loose your funk.
This steals from your power,
And makes you more like them.

Such is the way of the School of Haterism.

I say, haters hate because they hate themselves.
They mirror inner fears
Like an advocate exposing his case,

They feed on gloom and tears,
Making a sacrament of misery,
And a ritual addiction to jealousy and pain.
And they never take a sabbatical.

Take pity, and do not be vexed by their plea.
Instead, teach them to walk barefoot on cool damp grass,
And how to breathe crisp air from evening flowing wind.

To just breathe, and sway, and calm themselves
In the beautiful shadow of the tree.

Cover Art design by
Maleaha Duncan

Maleaha Duncan (2S queer, pronouns they/them) is a multi-media artist, photographer and published poet born in Fairbanks Alaska, home to ancestral lands of the Dena'ina people of the lower Tanana River. At an early age they moved to Oklahoma to reconnect with Cherokee family, community and friends.

Their artwork has been published in: The Morrigan: Celtic Goddess of Magick and Might by Courtney Weber and is also available in the Brookyn Art Library. The poetry title "Between Two Coffins" is a heart wrenching book about death, change, life, and expression at its darkest hour. This poetry collection is available on Amazon and Kindle. Maleaha currently resides in Tahlequah, Oklahoma and Iowa.

Notes

IT'S A NEW DAWN, IT'S A NEW DAY
Fatherhood; Rising to the Ultimate Challenge, Etan Thomas,
(New York, New American Library, Penguin Books Ltd., 2012).

THE NINETY-NINE
Voices of the Future, Presented by: Etan Thomas,
(Chicago, Haymarket Books, 2012).

REQUIUM FOR GRANDPA FREDDIE
Fatherhood; Rising to the Ultimate Challenge, Etan Thomas,
(New York, New American Library, Penguin Books Ltd., 2012).

About the Author

JULIAN THOMAS is a poet, audiobook narrator, acting teacher, and youth mentor born and raised in Tulsa, Oklahoma. His high school and middle school buildings stand just minutes away from the historic Greenwood District, also known as Black Wall Street.

Julian is the author of "Redemption Songs; A Trilogy of Poetry" available on Amazon. His work has appeared in numerous publications including the poetry anthology "Voice of the Future." Julian Thomas is best known for speaking roles in season 1 of the hit show "Hunters", and ABC's "For Life", as well as acting for several years in comedy sketches on "The Tonight Show with Jimmy Fallon."

Gravitating toward acting from an early age, Julian is a graduate of the renown theatre program at Northwestern University and has performed his original poetry on outlets coast to coast, including the St. Louis NBC news, as well as Al Sharpton's National Action Network. Along with a lengthy Shakespeare career playing roles such as Othello, King Lear, and Theseus in Midsummer Night's Dream, Julian has narrated over 20 audiobooks in fiction and non-fiction.

Among these include "Of Blood and Sweat; Black Lives and the Making of White Power and Wealth" by Clyde W. Ford; "Hack Your Bureaucracy: Get Things Done No Matter What Your Role on Any Team" by Obama Administration White House staff Marina Nitze and Nick Sinai, and Etan Thomas' "We Matter; Athletes and Activism", a collection of essays and interviews with high profile journalists, political activists, and professional athletes exploring the social justice landscape of today.

With deep family history in East Harlem where he now teaches and resides, Julian's Afro-Caribbean roots trace back to Sierra Leone, Grenada, and Honduras.

Book summary for Black Existentialism; Autumn Leaves and Other Space Oddities

The poems in this book present a mosaic of modern life that reaches back to the past to capture the pulse of the future. Tapping into topics such as social justice, economic disparity, spiritual philosophy, and most of all love, this book provides a compelling tribute to non-conformity and a celebration of those who defy social norms. Often set against the backdrop of East Harlem, 'El Barrio', New York, the poetry strides through complex intricacies of life and society with vivid imagery and introspective musings.

The pieces come alive with the rhythms of jazz and blues music, and immerse the reader in an artistic journey of creativity. To read these poems is to experience the culture. Engaging for ages young and old alike, Black Existentialism is a collection of writings that bridges landmark poetic influences such as Amiri Baraka, Sonia Sanchez, Gil Scott Heron, Allen Ginsberg, and many more, with the cultural vibrancy of the 21st century.